The Winning Woman

The Winning Woman

500 Spirited Quotations
About Women and Their Sport

edited by Molly Jay

RUNNING PRESS
Philadelphia • London

Printed in the United States of America

9 8 7 6 5 4 3 2 1
Digit on the right indicates the number of this printing

Library of Congress Cataloging-in-Publication Number 00-135507

ISBN 0-7624-0943-6

Front cover (clockwise from upper left):
1. Speed skater Bonnie Blair; © Wally McNamee/Corbis
2. Tennis player, Venus Williams; © Reuters New Media, Inc./Corbis
3. Swimmer; © Corbis
4. Florence Griffith Joyner winning the Olympic 100 meter; © Wally
   McNamee/Corbis

Back cover (from left)
1. Skier, Picabo Street; © Jerome Prevost;TempSport/Corbis
2. USA Women's Soccer team celebrates Gold at the PanAm Games;
   © Reuters New Media, Inc./Corbis

Back cover flap
1. USA Gymnast Shannon Miller at the Olympic Trials; © Reuters
   New Media, Inc./Corbis

Cover design by Corinda Cook
Interior design by Jan Greenberg
Edited by Molly Jay

This book may be ordered by mail from the publisher.
Please add $2.50 for shipping and handling.
But try your bookstore first!

Running Press Book Publishers
125 South Twenty-second Street
Philadelphia, Pennsylvania 19103-4399

Contents

Battle
of the Sexes

I'd prefer to see women compete using the same standards as men, even if it means we have some ugliness from time to time, such as off-court trash talk not rampant in women's sports.

MARIAH BURTON NEBSON, IN *EMBRACING VICTORY: LIFE LESSONS IN COMPETITION AND PASSION*

She's a great player for a gal. But no woman can beat a male player who knows what he's doing. I'm not only interested in glory for my sex, but I also want to set women's lib back twenty years, to get women back into the home, where they belong.

BOBBY RIGGS, ON SEPT. 20, 1973, PRIOR TO BEING BEATEN BY BILLIE JEAN KING IN STRAIGHT SETS

An old, obnoxious has-been like Riggs who can't hear, can't see, walks like a duck, and is an idiot besides.

ROSIE CASALS, ON BILLIE JEAN KING'S OPPONENT, BOBBY RIGGS

I've always said Bobby Riggs did more for women's tennis than anybody.

ROSIE CASALS, ON KING'S DEFEAT OF RIGGS

I kept thinking this was not about a tennis match, this was about social change.

BILLIE JEAN KING, TENNIS

It meant something because she won.

FRANK DEFORD, COMMENTATOR, ON BILLIE JEAN KING'S WIN OVER TENNIS STAR, BOBBY RIGGS

Before that, women were chokers and spastics who couldn't take pressure. Except, of course, in childbirth.

BILLIE JEAN KING, ON THE SIGNIFICANCE OF THE MATCH

It's hard to explain or believe how male-dominated, male-oriented, and generally misogynistic the world of elite sailing is. I've never experienced anything like it.

ANNA SEATON-HUNTINGTON, SAILING

I'll tell you why I'll win; she's a woman, and they just don't have the emotional stability.

BOBBY RIGGS, BEFORE THE MATCH

Women are brought up from the time they're six years old to read books, eat candy, and go to dance class. They can't compete against men.

GENE SCOTT, TENNIS PRO, ON THE LIKELIHOOD OF A RIGGS VICTORY

In most businesses, you don't come across sexism that is so blatant and just obnoxious.

DAWN RILEY, SAILING

I'm less concerned about women following in men's footsteps than I am in boys following in men's footsteps.

MARIAH BURTON NEBSON, BASKETBALL

The only thing I love more than hockey is women's hockey.

SUSAN SARANDON, ACTOR

Growing up, I had to play on boys' hockey teams. Maybe now boys will want to play on mine.

JENNIFER SCHMIDGALL, ICE HOCKEY

If I complain, I'm a bitch. If he complains, he gets air time.

LPGA VETERAN **LAURA BAUGH,** ON **TIGER WOODS**

Being successful as a woman—and I think all women can relate to this—you're constantly pushing the door to get it open. For men, it's wide open. We have to push with fists, gaining ground for every woman.

CAMMIE GRANATO, ICE HOCKEY

The Age Difference

She's no spring chicken, but she can haul.

DARLENE BECHFORD, ON 36-YEAR-OLD MARICICA PUICA, OLYMPIC 3,000 METERS GOLD MEDALIST

At eight I decided that I wanted to be the best tennis player in the world. From then on, it was always in the back of my mind.

TRACY AUSTIN, TENNIS

I am not the pigtailed girl anymore, but I hold her dear to my heart.

OLGA KORBUT, GYMNAST

We seniors have a new name. We're not veterans, we're not grand dames, and we're not super seniors. We're recycled teenagers.

DODO CHENEY, TENNIS

Kids have agents now before they even make it into their teens.

MARY LOU RETTON, GYMNAST

You have a gold medal but no driver's license.

OPRAH WINFREY, TO TARA LIPINSKI

I left my babies to go compete against girls half my age.

LAURA BAUGH, GOLF

By then I'll be 74–just two over par.

PATTY BERG, LEGENDARY GOLFER, ON BEING TOLD IT WOULD TAKE HER TWO YEARS TO FULLY RECOVER FROM BACK SURGERY

Steffi's so nice. And she's not an old person. She wears an MTV shirt.

JENNIFER CAPRIATI, ON 21-YEAR-OLD STEFFI GRAF

I was very young and I was experiencing my adolescence. The path I did take for a brief period of my life was not of reckless drug use, hurting others, but it was a path of quiet rebellion, of a little experimentation of a darker side of my confusion in a confusing world, lost in the midst of finding my identity.

JENNIFER CAPRIATI, TENNIS

I haven't wanted to dream the next dream until this one was finished.

ANNE ABERNATHY, "GRANDMA LUGE", AT AGE 44 IN THE OLYMPICS

As long as I am improving, I will go on, and besides, there's too much money in the business to quit.

BABE DIDRIKSON, GOLF

I've been in the twilight of my career longer than most people have careers.

MARTINA NAVRATILOVA, TENNIS

You see these kids with their entourages—fathers, coaches, people trailing the kids to wipe their noses and clean their diapers.

BUD COLLINS, ON THE YOUNG PHENOMS IN WOMEN'S TENNIS

Reincarnation.

ROSIE CASALS, ON HOW SHE MADE IT TO THE FOURTH ROUND OF **WIMBLEDON** AT AN OLD AGE

I guess that time has come to stop thinking about what comes next and start acting on it. It's hard to look in the mirror and say it, but at twenty-eight I'm a lot closer to the end than I am to the beginning.

PAM SHRIVER, TENNIS

Heidi and Lolita do the U.S. Open.

BUD COLLINS, ON **15**-YEAR-OLD **MARTINA HINGIS** PLAYING **15**-YEAR-OLD **ANNA KOURNIKOVA**

I'm only 14.

NADIA COMANECI, ASKED AFTER WINNING THE GOLD MEDAL IF SHE WAS
GOING TO RETIRE

Her idea of drug use is probably Flintstone vitamins.

MIKE DOWNEY, COLUMNIST, ON 14-YEAR-OLD OLYMPIC SWIMMER
AMANDA BEARD

We're so young, we decided to dress only seven
players on the road. We're pretty confident the
other five can dress themselves.

CHARLIE JUST, WOMEN'S BASKETBALL COACH AT BELLARMINE COLLEGE, ON HIS
VERY YOUNG TEAM

My body has pretty much told me that it's given everything it's going to give.

FRANCIE LARRIUE SMITH, ON SLOWING DOWN AFTER YEARS AS A TOPFLIGHT RUNNER

I act my age better than she does.

CARL LINDGREN, 84 YEARS OLD, ON HIS 86-YEAR-OLD WIFE, MAVIS, WHO HAD JUST COMPLETED A MARATHON

I guess you get slower as you get older.

MAVIS LINDGREN, 87-YEAR-OLD MARATHONER, ON HAVING SLOWER TIMES THAN IN PREVIOUS YEARS

Stop playing against the girls and start fighting against the women.

MIRJANA LUCIE, ON JOINING THE PRO TENNIS TOUR AT AGE 15

I'll be able to show people it doesn't matter how old you are.

SHANNON MILLER, ON BEING LABELED TOO OLD FOR GYMNASTICS AT AGE 19

Should van Gogh have stopped painting at an early age?

MARTINA NAVRATILOVA, ASKED IF SHE CONSIDERED RETIREMENT AFTER WINNING HER 10TH WIMBLEDON

The only thing I like about that number is that it's a good score to turn in for nine holes.

LISELOTTE NEUMANN, LPGA PRO, ON TURNING 30

It's not do or die; it's do or don't.

MERLENE OTTEY, TRACK STAR, ON HER FUTURE AT AGE 37

You lose a lot of speed between 80 and 86.

RUTH ROTHFARB, ON HAVING ONE OF HER SLOWER TIMES WHEN RUNNING IN HER LATE 80S

Of course, I can say, individually I hate them.

ALICE RITZMAN, LPGA NONWINNER, ON THE NEW STARS OF THE GAME

If you drive a Porshe or Mercedes at 17, what the heck will you have left to drive when you're 30?

PAM SHRIVER, ON LARGE PURSES FOR WOMEN TENNIS PROS

This is the first time I've fulfilled the fantasy of a middle-aged man.

PAM SHRIVER, ON BEATING A MIDDLE-AGED MAN IN A PLAY THE PRO CONTEST

I don't know where they're coming from, but I wish they'd send them back.

WENDY TURNBULL, PRO TENNIS PLAYER, ON LOSING TO YOUNG, TALENTED PLAYERS

I want to show people that we're not just a bunch of old ladies out there running. We're going pretty fast.

RUTH WYSOCKI, ON "MASTER" RUNNERS

It's hard to keep up with the younger people coming up.

KIM ZMESKAL, 16-YEAR-OLD GYMNAST

I guess I could put it on one of my jackets, but I think at my age I will frame it and put it in the hallway where everyone can see it.

VERA RATTS, 89 YEARS OLD, ON BEING GIVEN AN HONORARY LETTER FROM THE INDIANA UNIVERSITY SWIM TEAM BECAUSE WHEN SHE WAS COMPETING, THEY DID NOT GIVE WOMEN VARSITY LETTERS

What ticks me off is seeing how much the seniors are making playing on Mickey Mouse golf courses, shooting 20 under par.

HELEN ALFREDSSON, ON THE DISPARITY BETWEEN THE **LPGA** AND THE SENIOR TOUR

I don't throw up.

SANDRA HAYNIE, ON THE DIFFERENCE IN HER GOLF GAME OVER THE LAST **20** YEARS

America loves power. I'd rather see someone hit it 350 yards off the tee, too. But I'd rather watch us than the seniors.

JULI INKSTER, ON THE **LPGA**

Olympic Gold

Losing the Olympic record is kind of bad, but I'm glad I lost it to an American.

CHANDRA CHEESBOROUGH, ON LOSING THE 400 METERS TO VALERIE BRISCO-HOOKS

These Olympics, probably more than ever before, are showing a lot of little girls it's OK to sweat, it's OK to play hard, it's OK to be an athlete.

LINDSAY DAVENPORT, ON THE SIGNIFICANCE OF THE '96 GAMES

Trampoline is almost an extreme sport. It's a rush. It's the closest a person can come to flying.

JENNIFER PARILLA, 2000 OLYMPIC TRAMPOLINE MEDALIST

I could have won a medal in five events if they let me.

BABE DIDRIKSON, ON BEING ALLOWED TO PARTICIPATE IN ONLY THREE EVENTS IN THE '32 GAMES

The unity of the athletes was the biggest high. It was almost like we came together as one.

LISA FERNANDEZ, U.S. OLYMPIAN SOFTBALL PITCHER, ON THE IMPACT OF WOMEN'S SPORTS IN THE '96 OLYMPICS

The Olympics is an incredible opportunity, but it's like anything else: whoever wins a race is just having a better day.

JULIANA FURTADO, OLYMPIC CYCLIST

Where I come from, winning an Olympic medal is bigger than beating Martina Navratilova in the U.S. Open.

ZINA GARRISON, TENNIS

The sun was shining. Everything was there. It was one great feeling.

FLORENCE GRIFFITH-JOYNER, ON HER MIRACULOUS '88 OLYMPICS

In the history of the human race, a teeny tiny percentage of people ever have or ever will have the chance to say they were Olympians, and I just happen to be one of them.

STACEY NUVEMAN, SOFTBALL

I can tell you, as a guy, how refreshing it is to see women on TV swimming, playing tennis, and horseback riding and not telling you how fresh they feel.

JAY LENO, ON THE '96 OLYMPICS

When I stepped onto the ice, I knew what the Olympic experience is. It's a feeling of pure joy, and I put it in my program.

TARA LIPINSKI, ICE SKATING

All kids dream of being in the Olympics, not to mention in their own country. But being on Letterman: that's something I never imagined.

REBECCA LOBO, BASKETBALL

I didn't want Chris going to Seoul with all those strange men.

PETE PFITZINGER, ON MAKING THE U.S. OLYMPIC MARATHON TEAM AFTER HIS WIFE MADE THE NEW ZEALAND OLYMPIC TEAM

The United States is no longer a follower in world gymnastics; we are a leader.

MARY LOU RETTON, ON THE UNITED STATES WINNING ITS FIRST OVERALL TEAM GOLD MEDAL IN THE '96 OLYMPICS

It's not a dream, because it's something I never even thought was possible. It's something I wouldn't have even dreamed about.

PAM SHRIVER, ON PLAYING ON THE FIRST **U.S.** OLYMPIC TENNIS TEAM

I think the best show in town is the Olympics, and I go to lots of other events. But like any other red-blooded female, I'm sure I'll get there.

PAM SHRIVER, ON MAKING SHOPPING A PRIORITY AT THE SEOUL OLYMPICS

I'm staying in my first coed dorm. You don't get that kind of luxury in the women's tour.

PAM SHRIVER, ON THE ADVANTAGES OF BEING ON THE **'88** OLYMPIC TEAM

I'm hoping some of the speed comes up through the floor and suddenly I've found myself very agile and quick on the court.

PAM SHRIVER, ON LIVING BELOW THE TRACK AND FIELD CONTENDERS IN THE OLYMPIC VILLAGE

They see athletics as one of the few places they have a chance to be number one, where they are judged purely on merit and their sex matters not in the least.

PAUL WYLIE, U.S. SKATER, ON WHY WOMEN SEEM TO DO BETTER IN THE OLYMPICS THAN MEN

There's a rush of adrenaline from this. There's such beauty when she pulls it off, but there's that danger, too.

DICK STONE, FATHER OF OLYMPIC AERIAL SKIER NIKKI STONE

I learned a lot about life here: everything is not Cinderella.

DEBI THOMAS, ON FINISHING A DISAPPOINTING THIRD IN THE '88 OLYMPICS

They said it: "Competing in the Olympics is the highest point one can achieve as an athlete. Gold makes me happier than a world record."

KRISTIN OTTO, SWIMMING

It is because I have lived a most difficult life that I could do this.

OKSANA BAIUL, ON HOW SHE WAS ABLE TO OVERCOME BEING AN ORPHAN AND PHYSICAL PAIN TO WIN THE GOLD

It is never routine, let me tell you. Once you think it's routine, that's when it's going to be taken away from you quicker than you can think.

BONNIE BLAIR, ON WINNING HER FOURTH GOLD MEDAL

When I ask myself if I want an ice cream soda, I answer, 'Not as badly as I want a gold medal.'

KATHY JOHNSON, SILVER MEDAL OLYMPIC GYMNAST

I cleaned my room.

TARA LIPINSKI, ON WHAT SHE DID BEFORE HER GOLD MEDAL PERFORMANCE

I want little girls to be inspired by seeing that a woman who is not like a man can win in sports. I think my medals touch all women.

MANUELA DI CENTA, GLAMOROUS ITALIAN CROSS-COUNTRY SKIER, ON WINNING TWO GOLD MEDALS IN THE '94 OLYMPICS

Every time they put the silver medal around her neck, she would cry and be disgusted. She wanted the gold.

NATALIE GRANATO, MOTHER OF HOCKEY PLAYER CAMMI, WHOSE U.S. TEAM HAD LOST SIX WORLD CHAMPIONSHIPS TO CANADA BEFORE WINNING THE OLYMPIC GOLD MEDAL

I guess I'll always envision this as a kind of heaven, sort of a dream world. Only this dream world was real.

MARY T. MEAGHER, ON HER THREE GOLD MEDALS IN THE '84 OLYMPICS

I thought the best I could do was third place and now I am a winner. I think that I am dreaming.

PARASKEVI PATOULIDOU, WINNER OF THE 100-METER HURDLES IN THE '92 OLYMPICS

The gold medal outweighs the bear, most definitely.

KIM RHODE, OLYMPIC GOLD MEDALIST IN SHOOTING, WHOSE PRIOR HIGHLIGHT HAD BEEN SHOOTING A BEAR WHEN SHE WAS 15

I kept forgetting the middle part. I would juggle around the ramparts and rockets' red glare. But I think I nailed it tonight.

PICABO STREET, SKIING, ON SINGING THE **NATIONAL ANTHEM** AFTER WINNING GOLD

Everybody shared in it. I never stopped smiling.

DOT RICHARDSON, U.S. SOFTBALL STAR AND DOCTOR, ON SHOWING HER GOLD MEDAL TO ALL HER PATIENTS

I kissed it. I checked and I bit it. It's real.

JENNIFER SCHMIDGALL, MEMBER OF THE TRIUMPHANT **U.S.** HOCKEY TEAM

I just want to sit down and relax. I want to enjoy that feeling that nobody expects me to do anything great tomorrow.

SUMMER SANDERS, ON WINING A GOLD MEDAL IN SWIMMING AFTER HIGH EXPECTATIONS

I'd just show them my medal.

BRIANA SCURRY, MEMBER OF THE CHAMPION U.S. SOCCER TEAM, ON WHAT WOULD HAVE HAPPENED IF SHE'D BEEN STOPPED AFTER FULFILLING HER PROMISE TO RUN NAKED IN ATLANTA IF THE TEAM WON THE GOLD

No, none whatsoever.

JEAN SHILEY, 1932 U.S. GOLD MEDALIST IN THE HIGH JUMP, WHEN ASKED IF SHE GOT ANY RECOGNITION FOR HER ACHIEVEMENT

I'll never forget stepping up on the victory stand and reaching out for that fourth gold medal. The flag went up with the light shimmering on the water, and I realized I finally reached my dream.
PAT MCCORMICK, DIVER

I thought I'd like to hear the National Anthem.
LINDSAY DAVENPORT, TENNIS, ON HER MOTIVATION FOR WINNING A GOLD MEDAL

I wish I could bottle the feeling I had (from winning the gold medal); I'd be the richest person on the earth.
NIKKI STONE, GOLD MEDAL WINNER FOR AERIAL SKIING

It was just the way I visualized it. I mean, wow, I've waited so long for the National Anthem to be played for me and only me.

PICABO STREET, SKIING, ON WINNING A GOLD MEDAL

I think a lot of people get carried away with gold, silver, or bronze, but you've got to focus on doing better than you have ever done before. You've got to focus on beating yourself and understanding that success does not mean finishing first.

BONNIE BLAIR, SPEED SKATER

It was like a concert and you're on stage. It was too hard to fathom that all those people were looking at you and screaming.

DONNA WEINBRECHT, ON **20,000** PEOPLE ROOTING FOR HER TO WIN THE GOLD MEDAL IN FREESTYLE SKATING

The beautiful Olympic competition is about survival of the fittest. Strength is the engine of the performance. If you put a Chevy engine in a Cadillac, it will drive like a Chevy.

COACH BELA KAROLYI, ON HIS **2000** OLYMPIC TEAM

Coaching

Rooter. I am going to get some pom-poms and just get out there.

JoAnne Carner, women's coach of the U.S. Solheim Cup golf team, on her role on opening day

Here's how I'm going to beat you. I'm going to outwork you. That's it. That's all there is to it.

Pat Summitt, legendary women's basketball coach

No, Jackie, this isn't a coach-athlete thing. This is your husband telling you it's time to go.

Bob Kersee, asking his wife to retire

Playing under her is quite an experience emotionally and physically. She has an ability to get blood from a rock, that extra 10 percent when you have nothing left to give.

MICHELLE TIMMS, ON CHERYL MILLER

She is to women's basketball what John Wooden was to men's basketball.

DON MEYER, COLLEGE BASKETBALL COACH, ON PAT SUMMITT

I always cheer for my athlete, never for my wife.

BOB KERSEE, ON TROUBLES COACHING HIS WIFE

If that was me and I had a broken neck, I would have done it because this is a once-in-a-lifetime opportunity.

BELA KAROLYI, ON KERRI STRUG'S INJURED VAULT

I've got a headache, and I'm ready for a Stoli.

JOANNE CARNER, AFTER HER FIRST DAY AS COACH OF THE SOLHEIM CUP GOLF TEAM

My mother is a loving, gentle person. She taught me to be compassionate... I want to be like my mom off the court and my dad on the court.

PAT SUMMITT

Was he tough? You bet. Is he strict? Yeah. Does he have a demanding work ethic? Of course. But you know that going in. He creates champions. You go to him to come home with a medal.

MARY LOU RETTON, ON GYMNASTICS COACH BELA KAROLYI

It doesn't matter what he says. Take an ordinary sentence like 'Let's go.' Anyone can say that, right? Well, when he says it, it's just different. Totally different.

ALYSSA BECKERMAN, ON GYMNASTICS COACH BELA KAROLYI

Competing
with Confidence

A lot of great players don't win Super Bowls.

AMY BENZ, LPGA PRO, ON PLAYING MORE THAN **300** EVENTS WITHOUT A WIN

My biggest competition was battling the clock that was inside me. I felt that if I would overcome that, or do better than I expected, then that was whether I won or lost.

BONNIE BLAIR, SPEED SKATER

Competition is even more fun than golf. I like going down to the wire knowing somebody's going to choke and hoping it's not me.

JOANNE CARNER, GOLF

To me, to race is to go all out, every time.
BONNIE BLAIR, SPEED SKATER

Determining figure-skating winners is like judging
wine: you so enjoy the competition, you hope to
never have to make a decision.
DICK BUTTON, ON JUDGING ICE SKATING

People thought I was ruthless, which I was. I didn't
give a darn who was on the other side of the net.
I'd knock you down if you got in the way.
ALTHEA GIBSON, TENNIS

I attacked my weaker opponents more furiously than any other girl in the history of tennis.

MAUREEN CONNOLLY, TENNIS

This was no passing dislike, but a blazing virulent, powerful, and consuming hate. I believed I could not win without hatred.

MAUREEN CONNOLLY, TENNIS

It's just the playing, you being on the court, that keeps me going. That's what matters.

STEFFI GRAF, ON PLAYING THROUGH ADVERSITY AT AGE 29

Big boys, small boys, whoever—I was always ready to take them on. I wasn't scared of anybody's game.
CHAMIQUE HOLDSCLAW, BASKETBALL

I always feel big and powerful, like a draft horse, next to the little women on the starting line.
LYNN JENNINGS, DISTANCE RUNNER

Each point I play is the now moment: the last point means nothing; the next point means nothing.
BILLIE JEAN KING, TENNIS

When you're up there [on the leaders board], you win some and you lose some, but the fun of it is to have a chance in the last round.

BETSY KING, LPGA PRO

That's where I feel most free. That's where I can do exactly what I want.

NANCY LOPEZ, GOLF, ON BEING INSIDE THE ROPES

They don't really look at me as the woman driver anymore, but what devastates them is that a woman whips their asses.

SHIRLEY MULDOWNEY, CHAMPION RACE CAR DRIVER

Put it this way: it's much better for me if she wins.

MICHAEL MARX, ON HIS WIFE, LESLIE, A FELLOW OLYMPIC FENCER

I think the difference between me and other guys is that a lot of them don't have, truly don't have, the kick-ass attitude.

SHIRLEY MULDOWNEY, RACE CAR DRIVER

When I stopped competing ... I started venturing into other areas. I looked at my husband, and I'd be like, 'I can make a pancake bigger and faster than you.'

AMY VAN DYKEN, OLYMPIC SWIMMER, ON HER COMPETITIVE NATURE

I am glad she is confident about beating me, but talk does not scare me. Do it with a racket, please.

MARTINA NAVRATILOVA, ON HANA MANDILOKOVA'S SAYING SHE COULD BEAT HER

I never think about anybody. I let them think about me.

WYOMIA TYUS, SPRINTER

When I get ready to swim, I might bite your head off if you joke with me.

AMY VAN DYKEN, SWIMMING

When I'm swimming against someone, I want her to drown.

JANIE WAGSTAFF, SWIMMING

I'm trying to think of whom I should lose to and why, and I can't think of any reasons why I should.

VENUS WILLIAMS, TENNIS

All of a sudden, I lacked that confidence and that energy it takes to be any athlete.

JULIE KRONE, JOCKEY

You know you're better than the other players because there are so many times when you're down 5–3 in the third set and you don't get worried.

CHRIS EVERT, TENNIS

Running provides the challenge that allows me to feel good about myself. How can I expect to do well in other activities if I don't feel good about myself?

JOAN BENOIT, DISTANCE RUNNER

It made me who I am. I was given a tremendous gift in terms of athleticism. Maybe it was because I wasn't so confident in other areas.

MIA HAMM, SOCCER

Just the confidence that comes with chasing a dream and having it come through will make you feel you can do anything.

SARAH TUETING, HOCKEY GOALIE

Big Heads and
Loud Mouths

It's all the time Tiger Woods, Tiger Woods, Tiger Woods. I am better than he is. I've been on top longer, and I am younger. I'm just better.

MARTINA HINGIS

You couldn't afford me, boys.

ANNA KOURNIKOVA, TO HER MALE FANS

It's human nature for people to notice me. If I had plastic surgery to make me look worse, maybe that would help.

ANNA KOURNIKOVA

I'm not a follower, generally the leader. Sometimes others might choose to get on that path, but they have to get behind me. Everything I want, I usually get.

VENUS WILLIAMS, TENNIS

She's very pretty, but I'm sure she'd like to change places with me. Everyone is making ours out to be a rivalry, but so far it hasn't been.

MARTINA HINGIS, ON ANNA KOURNIKOVA

I don't have to choose, I'll take all the records.

MARION JONES, SPRINTER

If you want to know about my ego, which is obviously big, it operates this way: every time you tell me I can't do something, that ego tells me I not only can do it, but must.

BILLIE JEAN KING, TENNIS

This is good. It shows that she didn't beat me. I lost because I made all the mistakes in the match, right? That means I'm a little better than her.

ANNA KOURNIKOVA, ON LOSING A MATCH TO VENUS WILLIAMS

I can do it all—hit anything I want. I feel no fear. I deserve every bit of attention.

ANNA KOURNIKOVA, TENNIS

I am the great Lenglen.

SUZANNE LENGLEN, TENNIS LEGEND, TO AN USHER WHO ASKED TO SEE HER TICKET IN THE 1920 OLYMPICS

I think I started a revolution. Before me, girls were afraid of cycling.

JEANNIE LONGO, OLYMPIC CYCLIST

To save themselves from embarrassment.

ISMALIA MABO, NIGERIAN WOMEN'S SOCCER COACH, ON WHY SOUTH KOREA WOULD USE FIVE DEFENDERS AGAINST THE OFFENSE OF NIGERIA

I touch everyone. Everyone wants to see me, and I don't blame them. Got to get a look at Serena.

SERENA WILLIAMS, TENNIS

I'm glad you're doing this story on us and not on the WNBA. We're so much prettier than all the other women in sports.

MARTINA HINGIS, IN *DETOUR* MAGAZINE

You can have a certain arrogance, and that's fine, but what you should never lose is the respect for the others.

STEFFI GRAF, TENNIS

People ask me, 'Why do you have to look good on the court? Why not just play?' But to me, whenever I'm on the court, it's like theater, and I have to express myself. Why should I have to look ugly just because I'm an athlete?

ANNA KOURNIKOVA IN *SPORTS ILLUSTRATED*

I wouldn't consider myself cocky and arrogant. I'm confident and I tell the truth.

VENUS WILLIAMS, TENNIS

Do you want me to serve or break you?

MARTINA HINGIS, TO LINDSAY DAVENPORT DURING A COIN TOSS

I knew I wasn't going to be average.

CHAMINIQUE HOLDSCLAW, BASKETBALL

In women's professional sports, there's no room for divas. It's about blood, sweat, and tears. Basking in the glory of the greats? That's the glamor in sports.

TERESA EDWARDS, BASKETBALL

We Are Family

I just made spaghetti and told her not to bite her fingernails.

JACKIE BAKER, ON MOTHERLY ADVICE SHE GAVE TO HER DAUGHTER MARY DECKER SLANEY

I'm so focused on the game, sometimes I forget he's there until he says something in my ear.

SUZANNE BELL, COACH OF A JV BASKETBALL TEAM, ON CARRYING HER NINE-MONTH-OLD BABY IN A TOTE ON HER SHOULDERS

Raffle.

RUTHIE BOLTON, MEMBER OF U.S. OLYMPIC BASKETBALL TEAM, ON THE BEST WAY TO DISTRIBUTE HER FOUR TICKETS AMONG 19 BROTHERS AND SISTERS

I would like to see her retire now.

RICHARD WILLIAMS, ON DAUGHTER VENUS, AFTER THE ERICSSON OPEN 2000

She can hang out with the other mom—and she won't have to wear a parka.

BRANDI CHASTAIN, URGING DAVID LETTERMAN TO HAVE HIS MOTHER COVER THE U.S. WOMEN'S SOCCER TEAM AS SHE DID THE WINTER OLYMPICS

I'm more of a celebrity than the players. The only players I'm not more of a celebrity than are Venus and Serena, which is really amazing.

RICHARD WILLIAMS, FATHER OF SERENA AND VENUS

There comes a time when it's probably not cool for your mom to be your best friend.

LINDSAY DAVENPORT, ON THE STRAINED RELATIONSHIP BETWEEN MARTINA HINGIS AND HER MOTHER

Jackie and Florence on the same track on the same day. I wouldn't want to land that on anyone.

BOB KERSEE, ON OLYMPIAN HEIKE DRECHSLER'S FACING JACKIE JOYNER-KERSEE IN THE LONG JUMP AND SISTER-IN-LAW FLORENCE GRIFFITH-JOYNER IN THE 200 METERS ON THE SAME DAY

I guess I'm going to have to keep the gym open longer than I think.

BELA KAROLYI, AFTER MARY LOU RETTON HAD A BABY IN 1995

She showed me her gold medals when I was a little girl. I made a bet with her that someday I'd make an Olympic team and win.

KELLY MCCORMICK, SILVER AND BRONZE MEDAL WINNER IN DIVING, ON HER GOLD MEDAL WINNING MOTHER, PAT

Just look at Reggie: he's a millionaire for being a jerk.

CHERYL MILLER, DEFENDING HER TOUGH TALKING BY CITING THE EXAMPLE OF HER BROTHER, NBA STAR REGGIE MILLER

They're sheer power. They're going to knock the crap out of people. They're going to beat you up.

NICK BOLLETTIERI, ON VENUS AND SERENA WILLIAMS

We get together for weddings, funerals, and the Olympics.

KATHY MURPHY, COUSIN OF BONNIE BLAIR, ON THE BLAIR BUNCH'S ROOTING FOR BONNIE AT THE OLYMPICS

I beat their mother when I was a girl in a tournament in Belgrade. Obviously, I didn't beat her badly. She managed to have three daughters after that.

MARTINA NAVRATILOVA, ON BEATING YULIA MALEEVA AND HER THREE DAUGHTERS, WHO WERE ALL TENNIS PROS

All these thoughts go through your head. I said, well, I guess I will be one of the few players that have lost to all of them.

MARTINA NAVRATILOVA, ON LOSING AT WIMBLEDON TO ONE OF THE THREE MALEEVA SISTERS, AFTER HAVING PREVIOUSLY LOST TO THE OTHER TWO

For a long while, my son thought only women played golf.

JUDY RANKIN, ON HER SON WALTER, WHO SPENT THE EARLY PART OF HIS LIFE ON THE PRO TOUR WITH HIS MOM

Flipped into the world.

MARY LOU RETTON, ANNOUNCING THE BIRTH OF HER DAUGHTER IN 1995

Well, all that's left for me to do is go find John Lloyd and start a family.

PAM SHRIVER, AFTER THE MAJOR UPSETS OF HERSELF AND JOHN LLOYD IN THE FIRST ROUND OF WIMBLEDON

It would have been great if all three of us could have qualified. I'll just have to go out there and represent the family the best I can.

HAZEL CLARK, 2000 OLYMPIC SPRINTER, ON SISTER-IN-LAW JEARL MILES CLARK AND SISTER JOETTA CLARK

It's like I only have to use half of my brain.

SERENA WILLIAMS, ON PLAYING DOUBLES WITH SISTER, VENUS

Fandom

People come to see you have a go. I reckon that's why they come out.

LAURA DAVIES, ON ALL THE GOLF FANS WHO COME TO WATCH HER ENORMOUS DRIVES

We want there to be a bond between the players and the fans like we're one big team. There is no separation between athletes and fans.

BRANDI CHASTAIN, SOCCER

When I hit my drives, I hear it pretty much every hole. I never get tired of it.

LAURA DAVIES, ON HER FANS' ENTHUSIASM

I like demonstrative crowds. People who pay their hard-earned money for a ticket ought to be able to make noise.

BILLIE JEAN KING, TENNIS

It's like a menu: they can look, but they can't afford it.

ANNA KOURNIKOVA, ON ALL HER MALE FANS

Sports fans in the past were predominantly men. But once people see us, they realize that athletics is changing, and so have the fans.

REBECCA LOBO, BASKETBALL

I'm not better than them in any respect. I might play better golf than they do, but I'm nothing without them.

NANCY LOPEZ, ON HER FANS

What was I–a Martian?

MARTINA NAVRATILOVA, ON FANS ROOTING FOR CHRIS EVERT AND AGAINST HER DURING A WIMBLEDON MATCH

I'm the home team everywhere.

MARTINA NAVRATILOVA, ON ALL THE FAN APPRECIATION AT THE END OF HER CAREER

Unfortunately, I didn't hit balls outside the ropes, so I couldn't go out to say hello.

AYAKE OKAMATO, LPGA PRO, ON THE LARGE NUMBER OF JAPANESE FANS CHEERING HER AT A TOURNAMENT IN SAN DIEGO

I don't mind that mine isn't a spectator sport. I do this for myself. In my mind, tons of people gawking at me just because I'm agile is an extremely dumb notion.

COURTNEY MARSHALL, DOUBLE BLACK BELT OF KARATE

There were people here?

SUZANNE LENGLEN, ON THE FANS AT HER WIMBLEDON VICTOR

Game Face

They should be bottled up inside. You want it to come out at the track.

EVELYN ASHFORD, SPRINTER, ON HER EMOTIONS

I know how to smile, I know how to laugh, I know how to play. But I know how to do those things only after I have finished my mission.

NADIA COMANECI, GYMNAST, ON BEING CRITICIZED FOR NOT SMILING DURING THE OLYMPICS

They judge you on your makeup, on the way you smile, on the way you don't smile. It's very personal.

PEGGY FLEMING, ON ICE SKATING JUDGES

This is not the Ice Capades. You don't fall on a double axel and get up and smile, and everything's OK, you know.

DOTTIE PEPPER, LPGA PRO, ON HER GRIM DEMEANOR ON THE TOUR

I am like a mussel sometimes, a closed shell. No one can get to me.

STEFFI GRAF, TENNIS

I don't need to act mean. Not if I do what I'm capable of.

JACKIE JOYNER-KERSEE, ON SUGGESTIONS OF HAVING TO ACT MEAN TO DO WELL IN THE OLYMPICS

When you walked in here you were beautiful. Then you got your hands on a rack of balls, and two seconds later you looked like the deadliest woman in the world. You looked like a black widow.

CLUB OWNER ,TO JEANETTE LEE, THE "BLACK WIDOW" OF PRO BILLIARDS

I guess if looks could kill, I would have killed a number of people.

NANCY RICHEY, TENNIS GREAT, ON HER INTENSITY ON THE COURT

"Nancy with the smiling face."

DAVE ANDERSON, ON THE ALWAYS FRIENDLY AND PERSONABLE LOPEZ

Winning is like going out and beating up on people.
I get joy out of that.

SERENA WILLIAMS, TENNIS

I don't have nerves.

SE RI PAK, WHEN ASKED IS SHE WAS NERVOUS BEFORE WINNING THE U.S. OPEN

Winning and Losing

Sometimes I think it's me, that I can't finish out the match. Then I realize most of it's Martina.

CHRIS EVERT, ON LOSING THIRTEEN TIMES IN A ROW TO MARTINA NAVRATILOVA

I think the whole game hinged on one call—the one I made last April scheduling the game.

PETER GAVITT, WOMEN'S BASKETBALL COACH AT MAINE, AFTER HIS TEAM LOST 115–57

I lost count of how many times I got sacked.

SHANNON DAVIS, WOMEN'S PRO FOOTBALL LEAGUE

Things got so bad I had to play my student manager for a while. Things really got bad when she started to complain to the press that she wasn't getting enough playing time.

LINDA HILL-MCDONALD, MINNESOTA BASKETBALL COACH, AFTER A 6–22 SEASON

Failure is feedback.

BILLIE JEAN KING, TENNIS

I'm not a machine.

MARTINA HINGIS, AFTER LOSING ONLY HER THIRD TENNIS MATCH

We did something we should never do. We took it for granted.

JENNI MENO, PAIR SKATER, LOSING AFTER BEING PICKED AS FAVORITE

It's hard to promote a funeral.

KRAN LAYDEN, COACH OF THE UTAH STARZZ OF THE WNBA, ON THEIR RECORD OF 8–22

I just can't beat you.

MARTINA HINGIS, TO LINDSAY DAVENPORT

We didn't get our kids prepared the first five minutes.

TRICIA SACCA, QUINNIPIAC COACH, ON LOSING A GAME **117–20**

I go out each match thinking I'm going to lose, so it doesn't make a difference to me.

MONICA SELES, TENNIS

I've bowled maybe 25 times in my entire life, yet every time I went up to the line, I expected to knock all the pins down. I always want to win.

BILLIE JEAN KING, TENNIS

Being successful as a woman—and I think all women can relate to this—you're constantly pushing the door to get it open. Pushing with fists to get it open, gaining ground for everybody, for every woman.

CAMMI GRANATO, ICE HOCKEY

Achievement is difficult. It requires enormous effort. Those who can work through the struggle are the ones who are going to be successful.

JACKIE JOYNER-KERSEE, TRACK

You find something that is larger than your life and you can take from that and put it into your life. There is such a bonding with people—trusting, sharing, and communicating. . . It makes your life much richer.

ALISON OSIUS, CLIMBER

I like weightlifting because it's just you and the bar. Nobody else can help you. I can't blame anyone but myself. And I had to sacrifice so much to become good.

TARA NOTT, WEIGHTLIFTER

We go out and try to make the other player work hard. . . When we go out against each other, we are like, I'm going to give you my best shot to help you out.

TRISHA VENTURINI, SOCCER

Winning is like going out and beating up on people. I get joy out of that.

SERENA WILLIAMS, TENNIS

But the role I like best is champion.

KATARINA WITT, ON HER PREFERRED ROLE AFTER WINNING HER SECOND SKATING GOLD MEDAL

When I think about my records being the best times ever, it's hard to imagine they're mine. It's practically impossible for me to conceive of going faster.

JANET EVANS, SWIMMING

When you finally reach the line and you go through the tape, it's just an exuberant feeling, something takes over. I get filled with spirit and so ready to share my excitement with everybody. . . It's all those hours, months, days of training, the frustrating workouts, the great workouts—it's all coming together at once.

JEAN DRISCOLL, WHEELCHAIR RACER

I thought at this point in my life, I just wanted to accept the trophy with some dignity. But it's just not my style.

AMY ALCOTT, GOLF

Thank God the opportunities were there at the right time. You prepare hard at it, you practice. You shoot your best shot.

LYNETTE WOODARD, BASKETBALL

If you have pride in your game, you don't let opponents determine how you play.

TARA VAN DERVEER, OLYMPIC BASKETBALL COACH

My ambition is to play perfect tennis. Then I will always win.

MAUREEN CONNOLLY, TENNIS

I'm out to beat everybody in sight, and that is just what I'm going to do.

BABE DIDRIKSON, GOLF

I don't want to win every time. There would be nowhere to go but down.

KIM BARNES, WATER POLO

When I race, my opponents are my opponents. If it were my best friend, once we were in the water, it would be an opponent. I just swim to swim.

JANET EVANS, SWIMMING

Once you've been number one, you can never be satisfied with less.

CHRIS EVERT, TENNIS

Being a champ is all well and good, but you can't eat a crown.

ALTHEA GIBSON, TENNIS

I know what I have to do, and I'm going to do whatever it takes. If I do it, I'll come out a winner, and it doesn't matter what anyone else does.
FLORENCE GRIFFITH-JOYNER, TRACK

Whenever I hear anyone call me champ, I think there's something behind it.
ALTHEA GIBSON, TENNIS

When I lose a match, I know that I lose on court and not in life.
GABRIELA SABATINI, VOLLEYBALL

Chauvinists, Critics, and Cheaters

A woman's body shouldn't be hit in the stomach. Women's bodies are meant to reproduce.

EMANUEL STEWART ON WOMEN BOXERS

My wife is a real housewife. She cooks, cleans, and takes care of our children. She sews and knits their clothes.

HUSBAND OF FANNY BLANKERS-KOEN, SPRINTER, WINNER OF FOUR GOLD MEDALS

I step up and embrace (critics), because it's just another challenge. It fuels my fire.

SHANNON MILLER, CANADIAN WOMEN'S HOCKEY COACH, ON HER MANY CRITICS

Two sets of rubbish that last only half an hour.
PAT CASH, TENNIS PRO, ON WOMEN'S TENNIS

There is no girl living who can manage to look anything but awful during the process of some strenuous game played on a hot day.
PAUL GALLICO, SPORTSWRITER, 1936

Martina couldn't even beat her own coach. If Estep came back on tour, he'd be ranked 2,000.
VITAS GERULAITIS, ON MARTINA NAVRATILOVA

You can bet your ass if you have women around—
and I've talked to psychiatrists about this—
you aren't going to be worth a damn. . . Man has
to dominate.

WOODY HAYES, ON OBERLIN COLLEGE ADOPTING A WOMEN'S SPORTS PROGRAM

They pushed me away like I wasn't there. My coach
says, 'You are like a girl.'

ARTURAS KARNISHOVAS, ON BEING DOMINATED IN BASKETBALL BY THE OLYMPIC DREAM TEAM

It's the boxers who attract the real women, after all, with their raw primeval strength, beautifully toned bodies, and just a touch of vulnerability.

EAMON MCCABE, BRITISH JOURNALIST

I'm not sure the men would really know the women's game. I mean, how do you know exactly how the women are feeling certain times of the month?

JOHN MCENROE, ON MEN ANNOUNCING WOMEN'S TENNIS

I think women are too emotional to be any good around the greens in the clutch.

BOB ROSBURG, FORMER GOLF PRO

I haven't watched women's tennis in twenty years, and I have no intention to watch for the next 20.

ION TIRIAC, FORMER TENNIS PRO

Men are made differently than women. Men compete, get along, and move on, with few emotions. But women break down, get emotional.

MIKE TRANGHESE, BASKETBALL COMMISSIONER

Listen, I like to go out with chicks as much as anybody. Maybe more. But I didn't see too many in the league I'd date.

BUTCH VAN BREDA KOFF, FORMER WNBA COACH

I feel like I was stopped on the highway, robbed, kicked in the mouth, and then you go home naked.

BELA KAROLYI, ATTRIBUTING HIS TEAM'S LOSS TO CHEATING JUDGES

Why don't you just join the men's circuit and leave us alone.

CHRIS EVERT ON NAVRATILOVA

A wild colt. I've given up trying to rein her in. The girl's like a goddamn Dennis Rodman.

VIC BRADEN ON ANNA KOURNIKOVA

She loves the spotlight. Her attitude toward everybody else is 'peel me a grape.'

MARY CARILLO, ON ANNA KOURNIKOVA

It sounds like she's wringing the neck of a Christmas goose.

TED TINLING, ON SELES' GRUNTS

I'll tell you why I'll win: she's a woman, and they just don't have the emotional stability.
BOBBY RIGGS, ON BILLIE JEAN KING

Actually, the person who stands out the most in my mind for jerky behavior is me.
PAM SHRIVER, TENNIS

When we complain about conditions, we're just bitches. But when the men complain, people think, 'Well, it really must be hard.'
BETSY KING, GOLF

In the post-Tonya era, figure skating has become disfigure skating.

TONY KORNHEISER, COLUMNIST

Maybe our students had better take martial arts and figure skating at the same time.

FRANK CARROLL, MICHELLE KWAN'S COACH, ON TONYA HARDING

I don't really care what you think. I have my agenda. I've made my deposits. Now it's time to reap the rewards.

STACY ALEXANDER, DOWNHILL SLALOM RACER, ON HER ECCENTRIC LOOKS

How does he know? He doesn't have any.

NANCY LOPEZ, ON **BEN WRIGHT'S** COMMENT THAT WOMEN GOLFERS ARE HANDICAPPED BY THEIR BOOBS

She's always been a pugnacious SOB, but she doesn't have the speed or strength to compete with the men.

AL LEWIS, ON BASKETBALL GREAT **NANCY LIEBERMAN**

People should get over the fact that we play at the beach and should look at our athleticism. I'd love to see people who mock the sport get out there and try it.

JENNIFER JOHNSON-JORDAN, BEACH VOLLEYBALL

I Am Woman,
Hear Me Roar

Every day I struggle with my femininity. Boxing is such a boy's club—I'm constantly on guard. It's taken a lot of work, but I finally feel that what makes me a woman is what gives me my power.

LUCIA RIJKER, BOXER

I'm becoming comfortable with who I am and the way I look. I like my muscles now. I look this way for a reason; my body has a purpose—it helps me achieve my goals.

JENNY THOMPSON, SWIMMING

It makes me cringe to think of parents telling their girls that they shouldn't play sports because it's not an attractive thing to do and they should be doing feminine things.

JULIE FOUDY, SOCCER

Lisa's dominating and physical, and then, after the game is over, she transforms into this stunning woman.

JAMES WORTHY, BASKETBALL PLAYER. ON **LISA LESLIE**

It's okay for a woman to perspire. I still like flowers.
JULIE INKSTER, GOLF

Too many people hold fast to the old image of female jocks. They have trouble with seeing female athletes as feminine and beautiful. Something unique has to be done.
AMY ACUFF, ON WEARING FUR DURING HIGH JUMPS

I try to combine the qualities of masculine and feminine. If I can be aggressive and cooperative, I can do really well.

MISSY GIOVE, DOWNHILL MOUNTAIN BIKE RACER

In women's sports they don't even ask about your boyfriend. It's as if they assume that since female athletes are strong, they must be asexual. We are strong, but that's what makes us beautiful.

JENNY THOMPSON, SWIMMING

If she loves sports, she should be able to play sports and not have the peer pressure to be the cheerleader or barbie girl. I think you can be a great lady and also be a sports person.

JULI INKSTER, GOLF

We're women who like to knock people's heads off and then put on a skirt and go dancing.

BRANDI CHASTAIN, SOCCER

Oprah Winfrey invited the 1996 U.S. women's softball team to her show, gave them all makeovers, put them all in heels and fancy dresses, then asked the studio audience to compare their gussied-up appearance to shots of them playing softball, as if their skills were excusable only because they cleaned up so nice.

EXCERPTED FROM WWW.GIRLJOCK.COM

If someone says it's not feminine, I say screw it.

ROSY CASALS, TENNIS

I'm more powerful because I'm feminine; I don't wear my muscles. It's inner and that makes me invisibly fierce.

ASHLEY HORNER, LACROSSE

It is slowly becoming acceptable for a woman to sweat, work, fight, and show tears, but still play with the guts and resolve of a man.

LISA FERNANDEZ, SOFTBALL

I don't think being an athlete is unfeminine. I think of it as a kind of grace.

JACKIE JOYNER-KERSEE

I don't know if they expect me to be some guy-girl or huge person. I never thought of myself as a tomboy. I'm just a girl who likes sports.

SHANNON DUNN, SNOWBOARDER

Once I got older, I learned that I could wear make-up and dresses and still play basketball. It's okay to be on the court and be pretty. It's okay to be strong and shop at the mall.

SHERYL SWOOPES, BASKETBALL

When I'm playing, I'll sweat and talk trash. However, off the court, I'm lipstick, heels, and short skirts.

LISA LESLIE, BASKETBALL

I like to run like a man. I don't like to look like a man.

FLORENCE GRIFFITH-JOYNER, TRACK

I never consciously thought, Hey, I want to be an athlete instead of a foo-foo girl. We're strong and we have muscles. I think that's pretty damn sexy.

STACY DRAGILA, POLE VAULTER

We just have to keep chipping away at convention.
We will get there.

LIZ MASAKAYAN, VOLLEYBALL

The big difference is I'm showered and clean when
I'm modeling. The point is, I'm a woman, always.

LISA LESLIE, ON BEING BOTH A BASKETBALL STAR AND A PROFESSIONAL MODEL

I wanted a sport where I could still be considered
feminine. That hasn't been easy. Hopefully, no
longer are we regarded as muscle-bound
Amazonian jerks.

BILLIE JEAN KING

People accept now that a woman can be aggressive and competitive on the floor, and off the floor be a feminine woman.

REBECCA LOBO, BASKETBALL

I'm just a girl.

MARTINA NAVRATILOVA, TENNIS

It may not be pretty but something is definitely working.

SHARA KLEIN, 215-POUND CHAMPION ROCK CLIMBER

There is a boldness when you declare your purpose with your anatomy, when size is your design, your weapon, and you carry your body around without shame.

ALEXIS ROBERSON, FENCING

The one thing I wanted to do was show women that it's OK to be competitive, aggressive, and ornery and still be very feminine.

AMY VAN DYKEN, SWIMMING

Going to Extremes

Toward the end of every long carry, a canoeist strains to spot the glint of water or the thinning of the canopy that marks the end of a trail.

CHRISTINE JEROME, CANOEING

I like the blood screaming through my veins. I don't like it just to pump politely.

CORIN FIELDS, BUNGEE JUMPER

Extreme athletes are the sporting industry's answer to our insatiable hunger for anything anti-establishment.

JOANNE CHEN, WRITER

My favorite BASE jump is always the last one
I've done.
MARTA EMPINOTTI, BASE JUMPER

Not everyone gets to see this. Many people would
like to, I'm sure. But few people have the guts to go
somewhere you simply don't belong.
TARON SAMUELSON, SCUBA INSTRUCTOR

I worked nine to five for fifteen years and I was
boring the life out of myself. Now I barely make
rent and I'm ecstatic.
STEPHANIE EMERY, WHITE WATER INSTRUCTOR

Those moments when I went from calmness to curiosity to worry to panic; I have always feared drowning. . . why seek them? Perhaps not only to have stories to tell, but also to make sense of the stories we already know.

ANDREA BARRETT, SAILOR AND KAYAKER

I accept the pain as a part of the sport: the injuries, the hunger, the cold, pushing yourself to the threshold day in and out, the agony of defeat, the sorrow of starting all over again, the fear of failure and success. For me the whole thing is a journey. I feel like an artist—every course I go to, I'm creating a masterpiece.

MISSY GIOVE, DOWNHILL MOUNTAIN BIKE RACER

When you get to the Olympics, a sport loses some of its innocence and becomes commercial. They want you to wear a uniform and that doesn't really fit with snowboarding. I'm worried that kids will make winning a gold medal their sole purpose. They'll miss the reason the sport was created.

SHANNON DUNN, SNOWBOARDER

There was nothing I wanted more than to beat the boys. But I paid my dues and climbed the ladder slowly, which is the way it needs to be done in such a dangerous sport.

SHIRLEY MULDOWNEY, RACECAR DRIVER

Memories are moments in my life that refuse to be ordinary. All of my dearest memories come from out here, under the sun, flat against a rock.

HELENA TATE, ROCK CLIMBER

We finally have the freedom to be who we are instead of trying to be like the men. We just get out there and do it.

ROCHELLE BALLARD, SURFER

Someday I might find an office job that pays me five million a year. Until that day, I'll stay right here.

ERIN FULLER, PARACHUTER

Out there, under the deceptively placid surface, was a world blind to gender. Though I was taught by men, I was formed by and subjected to the rigid laws of a seemingly lawless realm that treated me and every grazing ulua or marauding shark with the same equanimity.

RELL SUNN, SURFER AND DIVER

Sometimes I think about the danger. It's hard not to when I'm the most powerless thing compared to my surroundings. But I don't want to look back and my life and wonder what it's like to really be alive.

DORIAN PERRIN, KAYAKER

Legends and
Role Models

Some athletes today do not believe they should be considered role models, but I believe you don't really have a choice if you are a celebrity. So I try to set the best example I can.

SHANNON MILLER, GYMNAST

You saw her and you got the idea of what a woman athlete should be. At the time it seemed almost like she wasn't responsible for just her sport, but for all of women's sports.

MIA HAMM, ON JACKIE JOYNER-KERSEE

Maybe if Davenport got crabbier about it all, people would pay more attention to her. But to her everlasting credit, she doesn't whine, she wins.

MARY CARILLO ON LINDSAY DAVENPORT

I'm doing all right. I feel pretty lucky. Hopefully I'll just keep doing what I want to do. I'm not stupid—I will use to my advantage the novelty that I'm a woman. But I hope to God that I never exploit it. If it can do good for other women in the sport, all the better.

DAWN RILEY, SAILOR

Little girls need big girls to look up to.

TERESA EDWARDS, BASKETBALL

I don't see myself as a pioneer. I just see myself as someone who loves baseball.

ILA BORDERS, BASEBALL, FIRST WOMAN TO PITCH IN MEN'S PRO LEAGUE IN REGULAR SEASON

I want a little boy to say, forty years from now, 'I want to run like Marion Jones, not Carl Lewis or Michael Johnson.'

MARION JONES, TRACK AND FIELD

As a competitor and an athlete I think I was a great role model. I was very fair. I was a good teammate. . . I got pleasure from putting all of myself into it and knowing I had tried as hard as I could.

KELLY ROBERTSON, SPRINGBOARD DIVER

If a young female sees my dreams and goals come true, they will realize their dreams and goals might also come true.

JACKIE JOYNER-KERSEE, TRACK

Before, we were playing because we liked to play. Now it's more competition—I want to be Lisa Leslie, I want to be Sheryl Swoopes.

ADRIAN WILLIAMS, COLLEGE BASKETBALL

I hope, when I stop, people will think that somehow I mattered.

MARTINA NAVRATILOVA, TENNIS

She's got something figured out, and she figured it out before any of the other girls. The rest of us are trying to catch her.

POLE VAULTER KELLIE SUTTLE, ON OLYMPIC TEAMMATE STACY DRAGILA

You don't see women getting suspended from their sport. It's so rare and shocking when it happens. With men, who cares? So many of them are a disgrace to their so-called profession.

BRYNN CALLUS, COLLEGE SOCCER

It's important that little girls and young women have role models. I view myself and our student athletes as role models.

PAT SUMMITT, BASKETBALL COACH AT THE UNIVERSITY OF TENNESSEE

I will be unstoppable.

MARION JONES, SPRINTER

I've been waiting to put a diamond in my nose. . .
but I'm worried that I'm going to make it OK for all
the little girls to have diamonds in their noses.
PICABO STREET, SKIER

A lot of women compare themselves to me and
would like to be like me. They look at me and say,
'She can cook, she can clean the house, she can do
shopping, she can walk the streets.'
JEANNIE LONGO, BICYCLIST

Tennis has always been reserved for the rich, the white, the males—and I've always been playing to change all that.

BILLIE JEAN KING, TENNIS

My dad, despite his friends' heckling, was always supportive. When I won the gold medal, he wore it around his neck to show his friends. He told them, 'This is what my daughter does.'

LISA FERNANDEZ, SOFTBALL

I am often struck with the observation that the spirit of the young modern world is getting much more open-minded. Because of the media, the boundaries between people—race, religion, handicap—are losing their tendencies to act as borders of the mind. What we gain is a more understanding, tolerant, and ultimately humane planet–a planet with a far brighter future than one in which we live apart, isolated, and fearful of our difference.

AIMEE MULLINS, PARALYMPIC WORLD RECORD HOLDER

We were dazzled by her speed, humbled by her talent, and captivated by her style.

PRESIDENT BILL CLINTON, ON FLO JO

There's competitiveness—but we support each other. It's an incredible thing, how female athletes handle such powerful, conflicting emotions. We're aggressive, but when the race is over we're comforting and caring to each other.
JULIE KRONE, JOCKEY

Billie Jean was Joan of Arc in a mini skirt.
BUD COLLINS, COMMENTATOR

She's simply the greatest women's player of all time. You cannot say that too many times.
PHIL KNIGHT, CEO OF NIKE, ON MIA HAMM

Perfection.

DICK BUTTON, ON DOROTHY HAMILL

You know exactly what she's going to do, but there isn't a thing you can do about it.

ARTHUR ASHE, ON NAVRATILOVA

She plays by feel. All her senses come into play. That's when golf is an art.

CAROL MANN, ON NANCY LOPEZ

They have shown us that when we reach back to look for what we've always love about sports—teamwork, humility, and sportsmanship—it's still there.

DONNA DE VARONA, ON THE U.S. WOMEN'S WORLD CUP TEAM

Winning is not what life is about. My biggest attribute as a role model is not what I've won, but what I have learned about putting my life in perspective.

LIZ MASAKAYAN, VOLLEYBALL

The beauty of her was that she never changed. She was the same Flo Jo before she became a star and she was the same Flo Jo after.

JOHN SMITH, TRACK COACH

For me, a role model is about just being the best I can be and stretching myself and challenging myself as a woman in a man's sport, without trying to be a man in a man's sport.

LUCIA RIJKER, BOXER

The first thing to love is your sport. Never do it to please someone else. It has to be yours.

PEGGY FLEMING, ICE SKATING

My teammates are the ultimate motivation. They mean everything to me. They are the reason I want to be at my best.

JULIE FOUDY, 2000 OLYMPIC SOCCER CAPTAIN

Determination

I was very aware that I was a woman and that the Iditarod was a big thing for women, but I didn't want to be given any special treatment. I just wanted to be viewed as a musher.

SUSAN BUTCHER, DOGSLEDDING

You just heal up and get back on the next one, the good Lord willing.

EMMY ARNETT, RAGING BULLRIDER

Everyone is trying to put me out to pasture. Maybe I just haven't found the right field yet.

LONGO-CIPRELLI, CYCLIST

I believe I'm one of the best pitchers in the world. I know I am, as far as results go. But you can't live on your legacy. Every time I step on the mound I have to prove it.

MICHELE SMITH, SOFTBALL

There are ten really famous male surfers in the world, and one really famous female surfer. That's me. I want to ride the biggest waves any woman has ever ridden.

MARGO OBERG, SURFING

When someone tells me there is only one way to do things, it always lights a fire under my butt. My instant reaction is, 'I'm gonna prove you wrong.'
PICABO STREET, SKIER

In my preparation for the race I am focusing on what I can influence for a top performance and letting the actual result of the race come as it will.
RUTHIE MATTHES, CYCLIST

I want to go down in history as the fastest woman who's ever been on earth.
MARION JONES, SPRINTER

I'm still trying to be the first Brandi Chastain. I haven't completed that mission yet.

BRANDI CHASTAIN, WHEN ASKED WHO THE NEXT CHASTAIN WILL BE

I didn't want to cop out on my own potential.

DIANN ROFFE-STEINROTTER, SUPER GIANT SLALOM SKIER

The ones who believed in themselves the most were the ones who won.

FLORENCE GRIFFITH-JOYNER

Doing your best is more important than being the best.

SHANNON MILLER, GYMNAST

I always ran through fear of being beaten. It brought out the best in me, being terrified of being beaten.

SHIRLEY STRICKLAND, TRACK AND FIELD

While I'm lying there, my competition is out there getting better. That motivates me.

MARION JONES, SPRINTER

'If it's possible, I can do it' is the one ideal that most influences and shapes my plans for the future. I want to see the sport progress, but as long as I'm able, I'll fight tooth and nail to be the best.

JENNY THOMPSON, SWIMMING

To uncover your true potential you must first find your own limits and then you have to have the courage to blow past them.

PICABO STREET, SKIER

Our greatness and vibrancy is born out of having a dream and going for it alone if necessary. It is about ceaselessly striving for excellence and achieving it.

MICHELLE AKERS, SOCCER

Most gamesmanship, I think, is for people with inferior skills. If you're the best, you don't need it. If I were advising someone, I'd advise her to put her energy into learning how to be the best.

MARIAH BURTON NEBSON, IN *EMBRACING VICTORY: LIFE LESSONS IN COMPETITION AND PASSION*

'I can't' are two words that have never been in my vocabulary. I believe in me more than anything in the world.

WILMA RUDOLPH, SPRINTER

What determines a winner? It's if you can take the second or third-best horse and win.

VICKY ARAGON, JOCKEY

No matter whether something is "fair" or not, you can't let it slow you down in getting to your goal and can never use it as an excuse.

DAWN RILEY, SAILOR

There are so many new opportunities for women, especially in sports, that there is no reason not to try new things.

A.J. MLECZKO, HOCKEY

You hit roadblocks sometimes and you just have to continue to go with your passion. When you hit an area of rejection, you reassess what you're doing. Why did it happen? What can I do about it? Am I doing the right thing?

DOT RICHARDSON, SOFTBALL

Never let your guard down and NEVER turn your back on them.

EMMY ARNETT, RAGING BULLRIDER

If you want to be an Olympian, if you want to be a National team player, you have to do the work on your own. You've got to do it when nobody's looking.

TARA JELLEY, FIELD HOCKEY

The environment here is good for determination. Secluded. No cars. No McDonald's. No whining.

BELA KAROLYI, ON HIS GYMNASTICS CAMP IN TEXAS

Kids ask me, 'Do you wish you had your legs back?'
I tell them no, that because if I'd never lost my legs,
I would have never started to run.

JAMI GOLDMAN, LONG DISTANCE RUNNING

I think about all the times I was picked last at
recess.

KATHLEEN HALLOWELL, JUNIOR GOLF CHAMPION

Racing is a matter of spirit, not strength.

JANET GUTHRIE, THE FIRST WOMAN TO RACE IN THE INDIANAPOLIS 500